STUDY GUIDE
TO
LESSONS FROM
SAINT BENEDICT

Study Guide to Lessons from Saint Benedict

Donald S. Raila, O.S.B.

Sacred Winds Press
www.sacredwindspress.com

ISBN 978-0-9830615-9-5

Sacred Winds Press
PO Box 1
Augusta, MO 63332

This study guide is set in Adobe Garamond. Designed by Robert Slimbach and
released in 1989, Adobe Garamond is based on the roman types of Claude Garamond
(c. 1480 - 1561) and the italic types of Robert Granjon (1513 - 1589).

Cover image: Fresco at San Marco by Fra Angelico. Image released into the Public
Domain under the GNU FDL, courtesy of The Yorck Project.

Contents

1

THE RULE:
NOT A FORMULA FOR GOOD ORDER
BUT A WAY TO LIVE IN GOD'S ORDER

STUDY QUESTIONS

a. How does the monastic tradition suggest the establishment of good order in daily life?

b. What is the danger of seeking order for its own sake? Can we become over-attached to "good order"?

c. In what ways does God sometimes call for an overriding of human schemes for order? Why does He seem to do this?

SUGGESTED ACTIVITIES

a. Consider praying part of the Liturgy of the Hours each day to help to bring a God-centered order into your day. If you already pray some part of the Hours, consider how you might pray it more often or more devoutly and effectively.

b. Reflect on some incident in which God allowed your human sense of order to be disrupted so that His Kingdom of love might prevail. Recall how long it took you to realize that He had a better plan for you, and resolve to try to recognize and welcome His loving hand more quickly in future events.

c. Ponder some of the current sufferings of your life, and consider how God may be asking you to embrace the Cross amid these sufferings – for the sake of your spiritual growth and the spiritual growth of others.

2

SEEKING THE TRUTH THAT SETS US FREE

STUDY QUESTIONS

a. From a Christian and Biblical perspective, what is the meaning of true freedom? How is it related to our having been redeemed by Christ and to our letting Him take possession of our lives?

b. What are some of the threats to this freedom in the atmosphere of our secularistic society?

c. How does the *Rule* show that self-discipline and self-denial can be freeing?

SUGGESTED ACTIVITIES

a. Prayerfully consider some of the disordered impulses that, in some way and to some extent, enslave you and thus prevent you from being a fully trusting child of God.

b. Recall an incident in which another person helped you in a significant way to become free of a serious burden. Try to see the grace of God working in this incident, and give Him thanks and praise.

c. Think about how you might strengthen your prayer life and thus clear the way for God to transform you into a more faithful disciple of Christ. Consider whether you are able, for example, to be more regular in praying the Divine Office or in practicing *lectio divina*.

3

RUNNING LATE OR RUNNING TO GOD?
LEARNING TO WELCOME TIME AS GOD'S GIFT

STUDY QUESTIONS

a. Why is it spiritually harmful for us to let our thoughts wander from one issue to another instead of keeping focus on what we are doing at any given moment? What does the word of God say about such mental behavior?

b. What does it mean to "run to God"? What are the benefits of learning to respond to God's frequent invitations, even when they interrupt us and disturb us?

c. What, from a Christian perspective, is the meaning of time, and how does this differ from our secular world's attitude towards time? What are the meaning and value of *kairos* as contrasted with *chronos*?

SUGGESTED ACTIVITIES

a. Reflect on a recurring situation or an atmosphere in which you tend to feel rushed and thus lose your focus on God and on the gift of the present moment. Consider what steps you can take to begin to overcome the attitude of haste and frenzy and to be more attentive to the call of God, who often speaks through a subtle "whispering sound."

b. Think about some disciplines that you can practice in daily life that, with God's grace, might help you to live a more focused life without mindless rushing from one thing to another.

c. Consider your state of mind and heart when you drive a vehicle (or when you travel as a passenger). Let the Gospel and the *Rule* speak to you about the way you handle difficult or annoying situations on the road.

4

Contents Fragile and Wounded: Please Handle with Care!

Study Questions

a. What is the disposition of Christ toward people who are like a "bruised reed" or a "smoldering wick"?

b. What can the medical treatment of physical wounds teach us about dealing with other people amid their obvious and not-so-obvious frailties?

c. What does the *Rule* teach about dealing with wayward brothers, and what conclusions might we draw about dealing with difficult people in our families, work places, and social/religious organizations?

Suggested Activities

a. Consider some typical situations in which you tend to avoid facing you fragility and vulnerability. Explore the reasons for your reluctance to accept your weaknesses, and bring these to prayer.

b. Ask yourself if there are some people whom you find unappealing or virtually unlovable. Consider it is difficult for you to accept their woundedness and how the grace of God might transform your attitude.

c. Apply the Gospel and the *Rule* to the negative disposition that you may have (or had in the past) concerning a personal relationship. You might focus, in particular, on passages that speak of Christ's lavishly compassionate concern for <u>you</u> and then consider how that ought to transform your attitude toward others.

5

Roadblocks in Life:
Occasions for Death and Rebirth

Study Questions

a. How does the Christ-centered peace of a monastery (or of one's Christian home) differ from the notion of a perfectly problem-free environment?

b. How does the *Rule* urge monks to bring the peace of Christ into disordered situations?

c. What benefits flow from bringing our communion with Christ into our experiences of weakness, inadequacy, and vulnerability?

Suggested Activities

a. Think about an obstacle in your life that frequently causes you anxiety and may lead you to murmur and fret. Discern how the *Rule* and the Gospel can help you to change your negative reactions.

b. Consider ways in which your use of affirming words or your offer of generous help might contribute to establishing more peace in someone's heart.

c. Reflect with praise and thanksgiving on a past situation in which God removed a roadblock from your life or taught you a memorable lesson through your need to handle an obstacle in a faith-filled way.

6

Dryness in Prayer:
Part of the Narrow Road
that Leads to Salvation

Study Questions

a. What is the meaning of "desolation" in the spiritual life? What are its possible causes?

b. Why might it not be beneficial always to have consolations in prayer? Why might our growth be hindered if we were constantly consoled or hankered greedily for consolations?

c. What are some helpful techniques for dealing with desolation in prayer? What pitfalls should one avoid? How can one open oneself to spiritual growth through a proper attitude toward desolation?

Suggested Activities

a. Consider reading a book on prayer that treats the issue of consolation and desolation.

b. Ponder some of the lessons you can learn from facing desolation in your own prayer life. When you are next faced with desolation, make it a point to remember firmly that God is <u>not</u> discouraging you from coming to Him, although He may be asking you to make some changes in your life.

c. Examine some of the typical distractions to which you turn when prayer becomes dissatisfying or dry. Consider how you might begin to overcome this tendency and to cease resorting to unhealthy substitutes for grace-filled perseverance in dry or distracted prayer.

7

STABILITY:
FAITHFULNESS IN LITTLE THINGS

STUDY QUESTIONS

a. What are some of the "little things" that God has done in the course of salvation history, particularly in the Scriptures? How can we participate in these grace-filled events?

b. What is "stability of heart"? What passages in the *Rule* encourage the cultivation of this virtue, and how can these influence a Christian's attitude amid turbulent situations of daily life?

c. What are some of the ordinary tasks mentioned in the *Rule* that are considered sacred and, therefore, worthy of receiving blessings?

SUGGESTED ACTIVITIES

a. Reflect on ways in which you have failed to be "stable" through hastiness in some area of your life. Consider how you can begin to counteract such a tendency.

b. Think about some repetitive task that you must perform regularly, and ask the Lord how you might perform it with greater attention. Try to remember that, as you do this each day, you are participating in God's own work to the extent that you welcome His grace to assist you.

c. Ponder the possibility of devising a technique to help you to remember the sacredness of each task in daily life. Consider how you might better glorify God in eating, dressing, shopping, reading, preparing for sleep, waking up, cooking meals, or conversing with others.

8

BRINGING OTHERS JOY,
NOT SADNESS

STUDY QUESTIONS

a. What is the role of joy in the Paschal mystery? In what sense does God want us to "rejoice always"?

b. In what passages does the *Rule* uphold the dignity of needy, frail, and vulnerable people? What do these passages have to say to the typical outlook of our contemporary culture?

c. What are some passages of the Gospels and the *Catechism of the Catholic Church* call upon Christians to uphold the dignity of human life and to bring joy to the downtrodden?

SUGGESTED ACTIVITIES

a. Recall an incident in which you were called to sacrifice yourself to minister to someone who was especially vulnerable. Try to remember whether there was some experience of joy linked to the self-sacrifice.

b. Call to mind an incident in which, when you were needy, you were served with kindness. At least in retrospect, make an effort to rejoice in recognizing Christ in those who served your needs.

c. Consider how you might commit yourself to uphold the dignity of the unborn, the elderly, or other marginalized people through prayer, service with an organization, or efforts to influence government policies.

9

Detachment:
Leaving Everything Behind
to Gain What Really Matters

Study Questions

a. Why do we need detachment and self-denial on our Christian journeys of faith? How does our commitment to these values go against the mentality of our secular world?

b. How can Christ's command to deny oneself influence our approach to praying over Scripture? What should we be seeking in our encounter with the word of God?

c. What is the meaning of "dispossession"? Why is it helpful to remember often that we are going to die?

Suggested Activities

a. Consider what means might help you to become a "living sacrifice of praise" throughout the day. Examine your frequency of praying the Liturgy of the Hours. To focus better on the Lord and what you are doing, consider whether it might help you to say, at least inwardly, at various times during the day, "Lord, I belong to <u>You</u>!" (or a similar short prayer).

b. Reflect on the experience of the death of a loved one and on the lessons that the Lord taught you through that experience, in particular about detachment, love, and what really matters in life.

c. Discern what elements of your life ought to be "put to death." Try to decide how, concretely, embracing a Lent-like disposition all year long might help you to keep dying to self and rising to newness of life with Christ, especially regarding a fault which you wish to overcome.

10

QUIETLY ENCOURAGING ONE ANOTHER: NURTURING FAITH AMID TRIALS

STUDY QUESTIONS

a. What is the one genuine and ultimate "remedy" for our trials? What is our role in welcoming this remedy?

b. What is the root meaning of the word "encouragement"? Cite some Scripture passages that mention encouragement. How is it related to suffering? What passages in the *Rule* speak of mutual encouragement?

c. How does mutual encouragement in a specifically Christian context go beyond comfort and the alleviation of suffering?

SUGGESTED ACTIVITIES

a. Reflect on some incidents from the past in which you received memorable encouragement. If you did not at the time recognize the experiences as gifts from God, try to see them that way now, and give thanks and praise to Him.

b. Think of some people in your life who suffer chronically and might benefit from some loving encouragement. Can you do something to strengthen them in faith?

c. Think of some people who consistently deny themselves in order to be of compassionate service to others. Consider how you might benefit from their example even if you cannot imitate their specific type of service.

11

THE CHALLENGE TO REVERENCE
GOD, PEOPLE, AND SACRED PLACES

STUDY QUESTIONS

a.   What measures does St. Benedict legislate to ensure that the oratory be kept as a sacred place? How might these be applied today to churches and other places of prayer – or even one's home?

b.   What are some gestures and postures stipulated in liturgies that you attend that help the congregation to show reverence for God?

c.   In what ways does St. Benedict call for reverence for people within the monastic community and beyond? What might these exhortations say to people in our contemporary society?

SUGGESTED ACTIVITIES

a.   Consider ways in which you can nurture inner and outer silence when you are preparing to attend a service of liturgical worship.

b. Examine your outer and inner behavior during a typical religious service, and consider whether you can do something to improve your sense of reverence.

c. Think of some ways in which you might be able to nurture a spirit of inner silence in your everyday life at work or at home. Remember that such silence is connected with a spirit of joy, gratitude, and patience. Consider how it might be possible to make of oneself an offering of praise to God always and everywhere, at least gradually over the years, and what inner noises that, with God's grace, you need to quell.

12

CASTING OUT FEAR

STUDY QUESTIONS

a. Why is it damaging to one's Christian vocation to judge oneself as hopelessly deficient? How does fear (i.e., being afraid) hinder our capacity to grow in God's love?

b. What are some ways in which Scripture and the *Rule* recommend the casting out of fear?

c. How is it that our freedom from unhealthy fear should not depend on whether circumstances are favorable or unfavorable? Can distressful situations actually help us work at casting out fear and thus to grow in faith?

SUGGESTED ACTIVITIES

a. Consider a situation in which you were overwhelmed by fear and anxiety. Try to imagine how God was trying to pull you out of such a disposition, whether you responded well or not.

b. Meditate on several of the twelve steps of humility in Chapter 7 of the *Rule*. Reflect specifically how these norms can help to deliver you from some chronic fears. Consider how growth in humility and growth in trust are connected in your life.

c. Consider how you might deal with one of your fears when it begins to overtake you. Commit yourself to asking for the grace to surrender that fear to the Lord quickly and to welcome Him to grant you renewed confidence and trust.

13

SAINT BENEDICT AND THE CROSS: PUTTING ASIDE OUR OWN CONCERNS AND LEAVING THINGS UNFINISHED

STUDY QUESTIONS

a. Why is it sometimes right, in God's plan for us (as best as we can discern it), to leave a project unfinished?

b. What passages of the *Rule* help us to enter into the Passion of Christ and thus to grow in patience?

c. Amid painful situations, how is Satan involved, and what is he likely trying to do? In contrast, what is Christ encouraging His disciples to do?

SUGGESTED ACTIVITIES

a. Reflect on an experience in the past in which leaving something unfinished opened the way for God's grace to work in your life, perhaps to provide an unexpected gift. Pray in thanksgiving concerning what He did for you.

b. Ponder the meaning of the statement, "Anything worth doing is worth doing poorly" as it applies to you in your daily life. Ask yourself whether you have <u>ever</u> done anything so splendidly that it was flawless.

c. Consider some of the crosses that you currently bear, including those involving your imperfections and those of people around you. Resolve little by little to overcome any murmuring over these crosses in which you may indulge. In a spirit of gratitude, think about the blessings that come from uniting these crosses with the Cross of Christ, even if they are never lifted from you in this lifetime.

14

Aspiring to "Loftier Summits": Pursuing the Goal in Little Steps and Avoiding a Slide into Mediocrity

Study Questions

a.   Why is it dangerous in the spiritual life (i.e., in our <u>whole</u> life insofar as we relate to God) to give in to unnecessary compromises? Why is it important quickly to confront and oppose temptations to become lax?

b.   What are some passages of the *Rule* that stir us to grow relentlessly in holiness? What does St. Benedict imply in his uses of the words "run" and "hasten"?

c.   What is the danger of setting goals that are too high, both for ourselves and for others? How can we best nurture growth in people (perhaps ourselves) who are "fainthearted"?

Suggested Activities

a.   Consider whether having a "little rule" (perhaps based on the *Rule* of St. Benedict) for the ordering of your daily life might be helpful in keeping you faithful to Christian discipleship –

i.e., putting Christ and His love before everything else at all times.

b. Recall a project in your life that was accomplished through the taking of small but persistent steps. What current endeavor of yours can now be approached in a similar way? Consider, too, how the grace of God is involved and what spiritual pitfalls you might best try to avoid.

c. Reflect on a difficulty in your prayer life that currently besets you. Ponder how you might begin to overcome it, by God's grace, in small, persistent steps.

15

Conducting Ourselves with Patience: Dying to Self-Centered Demands

Study Questions

a. What are some passages in the Bible and the *Rule* that refer to dealing with selfish inner demands? When people tend to react impatiently to certain situations, how can faith in Christ transform their behavior?

b. Why is it that special graces seem to come when "everything goes wrong"? How can people open themselves to these graces instead of remaining stuck in self-imposed misery?

c. What does the *Rule* say about God's patience and its intended effect on us? How is the Passion of Christ connected with patience, both semantically and theologically?

Suggested Activities

a. Consider a typical situation in which you tend to become impatient and perhaps also demanding. Ponder how you might learn to overcome this tendency with the help of prayer, the Scriptures, and the *Rule*.

b. During the coming week, whenever your patience is tried, make an effort to call out in prayer the following (or something similar): "Lord Jesus, be the focus of my life right now! Help me not to cling to what my wild desires demand but to yearn for You and Your merciful love before all else."

c. Think of a person whose faults or other weaknesses challenge your patience. Commit yourself to taking some steps to accept the grace to change your attitude toward him or her.

16

ACCEPTING LOSS OF CONTROL WITH HUMILITY AND LEARNING TO PLACE HOPE IN GOD ALONE

STUDY QUESTIONS

a. What are some of the graces associated with acceptance of not getting one's way? In what virtues can one grow under such circumstances?

b. What are some passages of the *Rule* that address disordered situations in the monastic community? What do these passages reveal about St. Benedict's attitude toward the monks under his authority?

c. How can Christians see even sinfulness as potentially opening them to the wonders of God's love? How can humble acknowledgment of sins help one to "pray always"?

SUGGESTED ACTIVITIES

a. Ponder a situation in your past in which you learned, to some extent, to "place your hope in God alone." Meditating on such an event, determine how you might take some little steps in your present life to help to overcome your worries and fears.

b. If you are experiencing (or approaching) old age, consider how some of your losses can help you to welcome God to take control of your life. If you are younger, recall some examples of older people who have learned to "age gracefully" as they faced the burdens of growing old.

c. Consider some of the past or present goals of your life that might not be realistic and might not be God's will for you. Reflect on how you might detach yourself from unworthy goals and how you might learn humility by the struggle to become detached.

17

LOSING EVERYTHING
FOR THE SAKE OF FINDING CHRIST

STUDY QUESTIONS

a. What is the hidden blessing that can come from the experience of losing things? How is this search for hidden spiritual treasure connected with faith and the vow of stability?

b. Why is personal happiness no longer so important for those committed radically to follow Christ? What is a disciple to do with the "empty spaces" of life as an alternate to seeking worldly gratification?

c. In the *Rule* how are new novices and newly professed monks called to let go of attachments? How can this process be applied to lay people in the world?

SUGGESTED ACTIVITIES

a. Reflect on an incident of your trying to control matters too tightly and then suffering needlessly as a result. Consider an alternative way of responding more trustingly to similar situations.

b. Write down some of the things and/or opinions to which you are deeply attached, and ponder which ones you might be called to leave behind as "rubbish" in order to follow Christ more zealously.

c. Reflect on a choice of your past life that strengthened your communion with Christ even while it limited your options. Are there current choices that you need to make that might be painful and yet would enhance your fellowship with Christ and with the Church? Pray for a while over this issue.

18

THE GLORY OF GOD:
SHINING THROUGH OUR HUMAN WEAKNESS

STUDY QUESTIONS

a. How did the glory of God the Father shine most fully into the world? Why is it that so many people failed to appreciate such a marvelous manifestation of God?

b. What are some of the situations in the *Rule* that might enable monks to see hints of God's glory and to allow His glory to shine through them? How do these situations reflect and extend the life and ministry of Christ?

c. Why is it, from the teachings of the Bible and the Church, that God's glory often becomes manifest in the meanest and humblest of experiences? How is this phenomenon in accord with what Christian faith teaches?

SUGGESTED ACTIVITIES

a. Recall a recent disappointment in which you were tempted to murmur. Consider how God may have been prodding you to be more patient and to let Him transform the situation.

b. Think about some humble tasks that you have been called to perform and how cheerful obedience to the call to enter into such tasks might allow God's glory to shine through you better.

c. Consider a chronic human frailty that currently afflicts you. If it cannot be overcome by legitimate means, ponder the possibility of God's using this frailty to promote your spiritual growth and your openness to His graces for the sake of your ultimate joy. Pray over this matter.

19

THE SLOW, ONGOING DEATH-TO-SELF: OBEDIENCE IN LITTLE THINGS

STUDY QUESTIONS

a. Why is it spiritually beneficial for Christians to remember daily that they are going to die?

b. How is baptism connected with remembrance of death? What are the practical implications of our call to be baptized Christians in terms of daily "dying"?

c. How is the virtue of obedience (which is also a promise for Oblates and monks) connected with preparations for eternal life? Why is it important to prepare <u>now</u> for death and eternal life, in a calm and faith-filled way?

SUGGESTED ACTIVITIES

a. Recall an incident in which you were called away from your own plans in order to do something more urgent. List some of the graces that came from the need to surrender your will.

b. Consider some ways in which you can prepare spiritually now for the event of your own death. By meditating on some passages of the Scriptures or the *Rule*, consider how God may wish to transform your attitude toward death and eternal life.

c. Ask yourself if there is an area of your life in which God may be calling you to die to self-will and to embrace His will in a fuller way. Think about some everyday situations in which you can say "No" to self-will in order to open the way for God to work through you more effectively.

20

STABILITY VERSUS RESTLESSNESS: ARE WE STAYING WITH CHRIST OR FLEEING FROM HIM?

STUDY QUESTIONS

a. What are some passages from the Gospels that indicate that the apostles had to be healed of self-centered tendencies? How did Christ teach them to be "stable"? How, in His own human life, was Christ stable and persevering?

b. What do the Scriptures and the *Rule* tell us about dealing with the tedium of daily life? Why, in God's plan for us, must there be many "dull moments"?

c. What does the *Rule* say about the practice of stability? What are some specific behaviors that ought to be avoided if one wishes to abide in Christ more deeply?

SUGGESTED ACTIVITIES

a. Ponder a recent occasion when you gave in to self-gratification. Think about alternate responses in which grace-filled self-restraint could have kept you more rooted in God's will.

b.   Recall an incident in which God lifted you out of a state of weariness or restlessness. Consider whether you adequately thanked Him, and resolve to take some time today to thank and praise Him for this great gift.

c.   Consider a difficult task which you face currently (or faced recently), and ponder some ways in which you can open yourself to the grace of perseverance to carry out the task to its completion. Reflect on the implications of "multi-tasking" and on whether avoiding multi-tasking might help you to focus better on the one task at hand.

21

The Call to Hospitality

Study Questions

a. How is hospitality connected with listening? Why is it sometimes so difficult for people to make room in daily life for others' needs and concerns?

b. What are some passages of the *Rule* which speak of hospitality within the monastery, that is among the monks themselves? How is such "mutual hospitality" related to respect, patience, and love?

c. Why is every encounter with another person a sacred opportunity? What are some traditional disciplines that can enhance this awareness?

Suggested Activities

a. Consider some little ways in which you might be more hospitable to other people in your home or work place.

b. Recall an incident in which someone showed you gracious hospitality; prayerfully ponder the beauty of that incident, and give thanks and praise to God for it.

c. Reflect on some of your current daily tasks, and consider whether you are sometimes driven by desires for glamour, glory, or reward. How might Christ be trying to deliver you from such self-centered motives so that you might better direct your energies to serving Him and the needs of others?

22

SILENCE, POVERTY, AND WEAKNESS: UNDERVALUED TREASURES

STUDY QUESTIONS

a. What is it that makes us human beings essentially "poor" and incomplete despite all our efforts? Why is poverty of spirit a virtue especially regarding our relationship with God?

b. How can the practice of silence, both inner and outer, help one to grow in poverty of spirit? What are some of the invaluable lessons that can be learned from the practice of silence?

c. With the help of the *Rule's* references to silence, what are some of the expected benefits of keeping a silent heart in terms of one's relationship with God and with others?

SUGGESTED ACTIVITIES

a. Recall an incident in which you felt inadequate, ignored, undervalued, or underutilized. Consider how maintaining a spirit of silence might help you to welcome the graces coming amidst the unwelcome circumstances.

b. Reflect on a situation in which the intercession of another person relieved you of a burden. Consider how this event manifested the loving intervention of God, who so often works through saints, angels, and our fellow pilgrims on this earth. Pray in gratitude for such a gracious gift.

c. Think about some of the noises you hear in your daily environment that hinder your practice of attentiveness to God. Consider what you might be able to do to reduce these sources of noise, whether they be external or within your heart or mind.

23

CHANGING FROM EVIL WAYS OF THE PAST AND EMBRACING NEWNESS OF LIFE

STUDY QUESTIONS

a. How is the vow of conversion, as mentioned in the *Rule*, intended to lead the Christian to newness of life in Christ? What are some passages in the *Rule* that challenge one to conversion? How are these passages in harmony with passages of Scripture?

b. Why is ongoing conversion often painful? What passages in the Gospel, particularly the words of Christ, refer to the blessing and the pain of persistent dying and rising?

c. In the *Rule*, what are some of the ways in which the abbot and other officials of the monastery are called to challenge the other monks to keep growing spiritually? How are the officials themselves also challenged to keep growing?

SUGGESTED ACTIVITIES

a. Consider how you may be resisting change in a particular area of your life where God may be calling you to grow. Ponder what you might do to lessen your resistance to grace-filled change.

b. Think about a situation involving some of your family members or friends who may need conversion in some area of their lives. Reflect prayerfully how you might be called to pray for them regularly and, if possible, to give them encouragement to let go of old ways.

c. If you are not already doing so, consider making a daily examination on conscience to help you to recognize and root out (with grace) some sinful tendencies. Recognize this practice as a valuable way to seek forgiveness, healing, and new life from God in Christ.

24

Obedience without Delay:
Putting Aside Our Anxieties
and Finding Christ's Peace

Study Questions

a. Why is the practice of obedience without delay, at least as a desirable goal, an essential part of a healthy relationship with God? Why are grumbling and any type of delay to respond to God's call hindrances to spiritual growth? How is love involved in this process?

b. What are some ways in which the *Rule* urges the monk to "cherish Christ above all"? How can these be adapted to the lives of lay people?

c. What are some warning signs that a person may be entering into full-blown anxiety? What grace-filled response to such temptations can help to overcome them and guide one to enter into Christ's peace?

Suggested Activities

a. Recall a recent incident in which you were called to prompt obedience in order to meet a practical need. If you did not respond promptly and cheerfully, consider how you might have prepared yourself to welcome the situation with greater faith and love.

b. Meditate for a while on the verse "Have no anxiety at all" (Phil 4:6), as well as the following several verses, and on the personal implications for you. Ponder how such passages from Scripture and the *Rule* might help you to overcome your particular anxieties.

c. Reflect on the connection of mindfulness of death with prompt obedience and victory over anxieties. Consider some specific ways in which the thought of death and your dying to self-will out of love for Christ might help you to advance in your spiritual life.

25

STRIVING FOR SIMPLICITY
AND REVERENCE IN SPEECH:
A CAUSE FOR HUMILITY

STUDY QUESTIONS

a. How can excessive speech be an indicator of pride and also reinforce a prideful disposition? What remedy is prescribed by Scripture and the *Rule*?

b. Why is a Christian committed to "speak the truth in love"? What are some passages of Scripture that call for healthful, Christ-centered communication?

c. Aside from the chapters of the *Rule* that deal explicitly with silence (6 and 7), what does the *Rule* say about speaking with moderation and humility? How might these passages apply to people of the present age at home, at school, and at work?

SUGGESTED ACTIVITIES

a. Recall a situation in which your failure to communicate clearly and thoughtfully led to someone's being distressed. Consider what you can do now to communicate more truthfully and lovingly in similar situations.

b. Reflect on your own or someone else's discomfort with extended periods of silence. Consider what you can learn about humility and trust from such times of silence, whether imposed by circumstances or self-chosen.

c. Think of some concrete ways in which you can become more simple, direct, and reverent in speaking to others whom you meet on a regular basis. Articulate why such improvement is a dimension of loving others as Christ has loved us.

26

PREPARING FOR A HOLY DEATH: BEING PUT TO DEATH CONTINUALLY

STUDY QUESTIONS

a. As one grows older and finds the body losing its youthful vigor, what choice does one still have over the way he or she ages and approaches death? What passages from Scripture and the *Rule* help one to face death in a Christ-centered way?

b. What are some features of the "culture of death" in our society? How do they pose a threat to people's ability to live in God's truth?

c. How are a frequent remembrance of death and an embracing of spiritual warfare helpful tools in preparing a Christian for a holy death? How is it that one can, in a sense, already live in eternity?

SUGGESTED ACTIVITIES

a. Reflect on the story of Jonah and his struggle with self-will. Try to gain some personal insights about your own reluctance to give up what is precious to you, even when it is quite clear that it is the Lord who is calling.

b. Think of some concrete ways in which you can learn better to accept, with anticipatory joy, the redemptive sufferings of this life and the purifying sufferings of purgatory that will follow death. Pray today for a spirit of grateful abandonment to God amid sufferings, and enter into such prayer regularly when you experience anger or bitterness over sufferings.

c. Consider a past trial that helped you to let go of some element of your life to which you clung as nearly essential. Ponder how some of the difficulties that you now endure might be helping you to "die to self" and thus prepare for a holy death.

NOTES

NOTES

NOTES

NOTES

NOTES

NOTES

Made in the USA
San Bernardino, CA
02 May 2020